The Short Guide
to Sustainable
Investing

T0270830

Cary Krosinsky

Executive Director, Network for Sustainable Financial Markets

Lecturer, University of Maryland Robert H. Smith School of Business

Adjunct Professor, Columbia University's Earth Institute

First published in 2013 by Dō Sustainability

87 Lonsdale Road, Oxford OX2 7ET, UK

ISBN 978-1-909293-52-6 (eBook-ePub)
ISBN 978-1-909293-53-3 (eBook-PDF)
ISBN 978-1-909293-51-9 (Paperback)

A catalogue record for this title is available from the British Library.

Dō Sustainability strives for net positive social and environmental impact. See our sustainability policy at **www.dosustainability.com**.

Page design and typesetting by Alison Rayner
Cover by Becky Chilcott

For further information on Dō Sustainability, visit our website:
www.dosustainability.com

DōShorts

Dō Sustainability is the publisher of **DōShorts**: short, high-value ebooks that distil sustainability best practice and business insights for busy, results-driven professionals. Each DōShort can be read in 90 minutes.

New and forthcoming DōShorts – stay up to date

We publish 3 to 5 new DōShorts each month. The best way to keep up to date? Sign up to our short, monthly newsletter. Go to **www.dosustainability.com/newsletter** to sign up to the Dō Newsletter. Some of our latest and forthcoming titles include:

- *Promoting Sustainable Behaviour: A Practical Guide to What Works*   Adam Corner
- *The First 100 Days: Plan, Prioritise & Build a Sustainable Organisation*   Anne Augustine
- *Full Product Transparency: Cutting the Fluff Out of Sustainability*   Ramon Arratia
- *Making the Most of Standards*   Adrian Henriques
- *How to Account for Sustainability: A Business Guide to Measuring and Managing*   Laura Musikanski
- *Sustainability in the Public Sector: An Essential Briefing for Stakeholders*   Sonja Powell
- *Sustainability Reporting for SMEs: Competitive Advantage Through Transparency*   Elaine Cohen
- *REDD+ and Business Sustainability: A Guide to Reversing Deforestation for Forward Thinking Companies*   Brian McFarland
- *How Gamification Can Help Your Business Engage in Sustainability*   Paula Owen

- *Sustainable Energy Options for Business*   Philip Wolfe
- *Adapting to Climate Change: 2.0 Enterprise Risk Management*   Mark Trexler & Laura Kosloff
- *How to Engage Youth to Drive Corporate Sustainability: Roles and Interventions*   Nicolò Wojewoda

Subscriptions

In addition to individual sales of our ebooks, we now offer subscriptions. Access 60+ ebooks for the price of 5 with a personal subscription to our full e-library. Institutional subscriptions are also available for your staff or students. Visit **www.dosustainability.com/books/subscriptions** or email **veruschka@dosustainability.com**

Write for us, or suggest a DōShort

Please visit **www.dosustainability.com** for our full publishing programme. If you don't find what you need, write for us! Or suggest a DōShort on our website. We look forward to hearing from you.

....

Abstract

REGARDLESS OF THE RECENT FINANCIAL CRISIS, increasing environmental challenges, rising global social inequity and numerous incidents of bad corporate governance, the vast majority of invested assets (approximately US$150T) do not consider environmental, social or governance (ESG) factors in their investing considerations.[1] Socially responsible investing (SRI) emerged to address these challenges, but it remains largely deployed in negative strategies such as sector screening and continues to be a small investment niche, largely due to perceptions about potential underperformance. Instead, many of us have been advocating a more positive construct to investing with these challenges in mind. As advocated in a PRI (Principles for Responsible Investment) academic paper in 2009,[2] sustainable investing is 'an investment discipline that explicitly considers future social and environmental trends in financial decision making, in order to provide the best risk-adjusted and opportunity-directed returns for investors. By anticipating these trends ahead of the market, sustainable investing seeks to identify ''predictable surprises'' that can help ensure shareowner value over the long-term.' While such forward-looking methodologies remain a small percentage of SRI, many trends are underway making this more positive construct the area of the field to watch closely in the future, given its potential to create a dynamic for meaningful change.

About the Author

 **CARY KROSINSKY** is Executive Director of the Network for Sustainable Financial Markets, an international, non-partisan network of finance sector professionals, academics and others who have an active interest in long-term investing. He also continues to teach on this topic at Columbia University's Earth Institute, as well as the University of Maryland Robert H. Smith School of Business. He was a member of the Expert Group that helped oversee and create the United Nations Principles for Responsible Investment, and was Founder & Director of the Carbon Tracker Initiative. As a member of CapitalBridge's Operations Committee, he provided strategic leadership on data and analytics. He also built & managed the first global ownership database for Technimetrics, and provided related insight to Citywatch, and others with international ambitions.

At Trucost he helped produce the award winning Carbon Footprint study of UK portfolios, among other reports, and was Senior VP there until October 2012, successfully launching the business in North America, including developing the Newsweek Green Rankings.

He has written for the NY Times, WSJ, NPR Marketplace. Bloomberg and other global media regarding sustainability and is a leading interpreter of equity ownership. He was co-editor/author of *Sustainable Investing: The Art of Long-Term Performance* (Earthscan, 2008) and *Evolutions in Sustainable Investing* (Wiley, 2012) which expands on the positive investment philosophy.

Acknowledgments

THERE ARE TOO MANY PEOPLE TO THANK. One could easily trace again the history of SRI and find mentors and guidance that has been useful throughout, but one key mention is in order here. My wife Valerie Brown spent hours providing very useful thoughts, editing guidance and assistance, all of which was critical to get this text to its present state.

Contents

CHAPTER 1

The Challenge
of a Sustainable Future

IN MANY WAYS, there's one overriding problem facing us. We can only burn 20% or so of the remaining coal, oil and gas in the ground and stay within some chance of avoiding a catastrophic level of average global temperature increase.[3] This is the science that has settled upon something like a 99% or higher degree of certainty, and it is a loud ticking clock with ever increasing urgency. Yet, as we speak, we largely continue with business as usual, not only in our lives, but with our investment strategies. While awareness is increasing in the wake of Hurricane Sandy and other recent weather extremes, we are at best chipping away at the edges of what we really need to be doing to move to a sustainable society, without which there is arguably no chance for a vibrant economy of any kind.

Investing could be the mechanism that leads us out of this morass, yet most investment strategies either ignore this reality, or take a negative approach to the subject. This book will explore how sustainable investing could become a means of solving a variety of dire, urgent problems, and in a positive way for all stakeholders.

Other trends beyond climate change also stand in the way of sustainable, healthy economies. Recent decades have seen global wealth continue to coalesce at the top, resulting in levels of global inequality that are a severe barrier to economic vitality. I agree with those who suggest that markets need robust quantities of optimistic consumers able to buy robust quantities of goods and services, despite potential environmental constraints to growth as long foretold by the Club of Rome.[4] Further trends in automation provide an additional challenge to anything resembling the sort of growth experienced in the last few generations by Western societies.

Governance is also a vital consideration. Corrupt practices have always been a risk to the well-being of corporate and governmental bodies anywhere in the world, as well as to the communities they serve, reaching all the way back to the first public company, the British East India Company.[5] Yet performance metrics for C-Suite executives almost always do not match the needs of greater society.[6]

With all of these environmental, social and governance (ESG) barriers and risks continuing to emerge as increasingly urgent for society and material for business, can we turn these into positive opportunities? Can investing become part of the answer to the shifting global dynamics we face?

Across ESG factors, it is the environmental reality that is most dire. Drastic action is needed to avoid a variety of future problems, most especially climate change from accumulated greenhouse gas emissions in the atmosphere, and adequate fresh water for increasing global populations. Other environmental challenges from pollution, toxins and other forms of degradation loom growingly critical. Everyone knows the risks we face from our current and future energy consumption trends; the emperor has no clothes, yet no one dares speak of it or act, as the short-term economic implications are significant. Too much is at risk, too many changes are required. Yet change things we must, one way or the other. We seem poised to experience either great calamity from business as usual or radical transformation from current high carbon energy-based economies.

When given a choice of sorts, investors typically stick with the status quo, even in the face of such looming environmental limits and concerns. However, fiduciary duty suggests that asset owners need to act in the best interest of the shareholders they represent; to maximize their returns over time. For example, the California State Teachers Retirement System represents the pension investments of the educators of that state, managed in order to provide maximized paid benefits over the long term to retired teachers both now and in the future in perpetuity. As it turns out, pension funds such as these, along with other classes of shareholder, especially wealthy families and individuals, as well as oil-rich governments and their sovereign wealth funds, own the overwhelming majority of the world's largest companies. Such ownership has become an unwitting enabler of the status quo. Large asset owners often assume, rightly or wrongly, that they need to own the market as a whole, in order to ensure that they are not in violation of their fiduciary duty. What, however, if it is suggested that in the face of future calamity there is a systemic fiduciary duty that all asset owners need to live up to? Would that not suggest a global, coordinated effort to invest in the future we require, and what would that look like? I will explore this further in the Scenarios chapter. The opportunity here is to envision the future we want, the future the world's children require, as Stephen Viederman contends[7] to leave options open for future generations, and to start moving capital accordingly en masse. Without such a vision, we seem headed straight to environmental and economic disaster.

Can we alter asset allocations now, and on a systemic, global, collaborative basis to avoid the various conundrums we face before it is too late, or is the level of existing, well established infrastructure making it such that we need to consider drastic measures such as geoengineering experiments being funded by the likes of Bill Gates?[8]

One way or the other, we would seem well advised to envision a path to global sustainability, and to understand what investing needs to look like in order for it to become part of the future solution. If this sort of approach is indeed required, and if a growing body of investors and asset owners start to recognize this, getting ahead of this trend would be prudent strategic thinking now. One eye at all times needs to be kept firmly on the financial side of the equation – pie-in-the-sky thinking has often led to the formation of bubbles, which then get in the way of necessary progress (capital needs confidence and economic success of its own in order to succeed).

So let us dig in and see how investing could become the answer to what seems like an otherwise intractable systemic problem.

A quick review of the history of what is most commonly called socially responsible investing (SRI) will be a useful place to start – to see what has been tried, and to help encourage the more positive dynamic we now urgently require at scale.

....

CHAPTER 2

A Very Short History of SRI

ONE THING THAT IS PARTICULARLY STRIKING to consider, as we look back through the history of SRI, is how the history of business itself has been taught, or as is most often the case, not taught at all in business schools. It is as if the history of business started after World War I, the last few decades being all that is required to understand efficient market hypotheses and the like. Yet when one goes back a few centuries, what you find instead is the origins of business in the British and Dutch East India Companies. These first global businesses were owned by groups of shareholders in common, creating joint stockholder companies which often experienced wild swings of bubbles, booms and busts. Spend a few minutes and read through the 'History of Slavery' section of Wikipedia,[9] which makes for compelling reading. Slavery goes back as far as recorded history, and directly overlaps the history of global business, with investors gathering to finance trading expeditions to parts of the New World. Moving forward, the late 1800s were also filled with chaotic market stops, starts and panics; history is full of bubble formations, from the Dutch tulip craze right up to what was the recent first wave of cleantech. In his book *The Alchemy of Finance* (Wiley, 2003), George Soros held that all things eventually seek their true value. I am a firm believer in this. What then do we think will eventually occur to companies with large intangible risks hidden within today's so-called externalities? Although markets have found a way to ignore many environmental externalities over recent years, can fund managers and asset owners exit in time from onerous sectors that become suddenly uncompetitive due to market forces and potential changes in collective global awareness? Coal companies are recently experiencing this phenomenon, trading way below price peaks from just a few years ago, as cost curves shift and coal use becomes an increasing health concern on the ground. Environmental externalities becoming internalized is a new risk that investors now face. There is a long history of academic literature demonstrating that it is not possible to time markets, so when to get out of environmentally risky sectors and companies becomes a pressing issue worth serious consideration. The same is increasingly true of social issues as well, with capital favoring companies that solve problems rather than causing or intensifying them.

From SRI to sustainable investing

SRI has its roots in divesting from South Africa in the 1970s and 1980s. This was an important first success for the field, with SRI getting proper credit for helping contribute to the societal changes that occurred as the country moved away from Apartheid. This perhaps helps explain why the first wave SRI community in the US has remained primarily rooted in engagement and advocacy as strategies for change. Globally, religious mandates over time also account for the development of SRI to what it is today.[10]

I have urged elsewhere[11] that we reject the phrase 'socially responsible investing' as too broad. SRI is alternatively known as responsible investing, ethical investing, sustainable investing, impact investing and more. It can encompass everything from investments in alternative energy to funds with a religious mandate to portfolios that seek to get in front of innovation megatrends among so-called 'large caps' (the largest public companies). SRI also can involve advocacy and engagement. There is also the exciting field of impact investing, which in turn can include areas such as microfinance and community investing. There are also regional differences that manifest, and perhaps most importantly, differences in performance once you parse out these strategies.[12]

This all reflects the ongoing terminology war that continues unabated in this field, which might seem hopelessly confusing. However, it is actually quite easy to parse through this noise. What Nick Robins and I called 'sustainable investing' has both a risk and opportunity side, but needs to be executed in a positive manner for best effect, as we found in a previous book on the subject. At the time, we looked at all of the world's 850 publicly facing socially responsible, ethical, sustainable, etc. funds, and divided them between those primarily positively focused and those negatively focused. Positively focused funds outperformed the mainstream and their negative counterparts over the one-, three- and five-year periods that ended in December 2007. In a follow-up book we parsed through the many SRI studies that have been performed, and found when assigning these same negative and positive aspects that positive approach-based studies showed outperformance, while those studies that found otherwise were focused on negative aspects. Deutsche Bank's 2012 study (**https://www.dbadvisors.com/content/_media/Sustainable_Investing_2012.pdf**)

on sustainable investing found the same, inferring that any issues in performance were due to negative approaches. Yet, the majority of SRI assets remain deployed pessimistically, a legacy of the history of the field and proof of just how sticky assets and strategies are, even in the face of looming change. We also found that better SRI fund performance directly correlated with lower turnover (in the sense of lowest frequency of buying/selling shares), meaning that those that did their homework well and stuck to their guns, ended up the winners. This sounds more than a little like Warren Buffett, and in fact a buy and hold strategy is what passive investors seek as well – low cost ownership over the long term – and so what seems most sensible to consider is finding low transaction cost investment solutions that best ride out the sustainability transition that we anticipate will only continue to grow. Excitingly, Jacques Lussier, former Chief Investment Strategist for Desjardins in Montreal, finds recently that successful investing is a process that can be enhanced by sustainable investing practices.[13] Even if sustainable investing does not offer 'alpha' (outperformance against benchmarks), if the practice does not take away from portfolio performance, then given long-term systemic fiduciary responsibilities there is no excuse for large asset owners not to participate.

....

CHAPTER 3

Best Practices in Sustainable Investing

IF QUALITY SUSTAINABLE INVESTING does not take away from perform-ance, while offering a chance for alpha, a quick review of some of the better practices on offer is called for. In the UK, and Europe more broadly, more sophisticated strategies continue to emerge that attempt to address macro-issues of sustainability as categories of opportunity. European investors have long been ahead of this game, and corporates are starting to see that if they drive sustainability a growing base of investors will be interested in riding this wave, in effect creating the sort of positive dynamic we seek.

Some of the most successful[14] strategies in this regard range from the Jupiter Ecology Fund to the UK's Generation Investment Management, the latter managing over US$6B, and has found outperformance over time through a combination of business and management quality as overseen by Al Gore and David Blood.

I highly recommend you seek out the Harvard Business School case study on Generation Investment Management, which remains seminal.[15] It lays out the investment methodology they pursue, seeking to evaluate companies on the basis of both BQ (business quality) and MG (management quality) with an underlying environmental and social sustainability theme. In effect, Generation Investment Management seeks and has largely found outperformance through identifying a small number of 'winners of tomorrow' with a sustainability lens, through factors that include market position, ability to execute and those that can solve societal problems. In fact, Generation Investment Management's performance would be even better if not for Al Gore's board positions at Apple and Google, which due to conflict of interest they do not invest in, thus preventing them from being owners in two of the best performers from a sustainability perspective. At any rate, Generation Investment Management's performance has been stellar, and they stand as an example of how to invest in a forward-looking sustainable manner.

The Jupiter Ecology Fund may be the longest standing example of what we talk about as future focused sustainable investing. The fund has a clear remit to find companies best positioned to solve environmental and social problems, and has had very low turnover of investment personnel over time as well. While struggling after the financial crisis, the fund remains ahead of both its sector and benchmark over the past 10 years, and has had a very consistent focus. For example, one of the top holdings of the fund for this 10-year period has been Cranswick plc, a provider of organic pork products. Other companies in the top 10 include Stantec (water solutions and more) and East Japan Railway, and although a UK-based fund, Jupiter Ecology has over 40% of its investment in North America.[16]

While both Generation Investment Management and Jupiter Ecology are UK-based and longstanding examples of SRI funds seeking positive solutions with success over time, SRI strategies that seek outperformance through opportunity are less prevalent in the US, where approaches remain largely focused on engagement and negative screening.[17] There are a handful of exceptions and they are worth noting.

Seeking outperformance through opportunity

Parnassus Investments based in San Francisco has been the most rapidly growing SRI fund manager in the US, growing from US$1B to 6B in assets under management in recent years, largely by taking a relatively sophisticated approach to seeking value through ESG factors. Parnassus Equity & Income Fund is the largest publicly traded SRI fund in the US as of the end of 2012,[18] and is well over benchmark for the last five years: +5.16% versus +1.34%. This fund has been the fastest growing SRI fund over the previous five years, which was quite a volatile period for markets, demonstrating the resilience of this approach. Examples of some of their largest investments include a variety of companies looking to capitalize on sustainability as an ongoing business opportunity, including largest holding Procter & Gamble, who famously pinpointed water heating for laundry as the largest component of their ecological footprint, and targeted it with cold water laundering solutions. Other key investments include Waste Management and Google, both among companies taking sustainability opportunities very seriously.[19]

Portfolio 21 is another manager that has attempted to find positive opportunities through sustainability, and they continue to be headed in a strong opportunity-focused direction. 'Investing at the Edge of Ecological Limits' has become their catchphrase, and they have outperformed mainstream benchmarks since their inception in 1999 with an approach that is designed to be low turnover, across companies of varying market caps, seeking companies 'designing environmentally superior products, using renewable energy, and developing efficient production techniques'.[20] During this same period of a dozen or so years, and while

Portfolio 21 has outperformed its benchmark, investors have chased crazes from the tech bubble to hedge funds and more. Transaction costs have been high for such approaches, while SRI strategies such as these get more sophisticated and refined, providing clearer solutions for those seeking the positive change we require.[21]

From a corporate perspective, if you are located in Europe, fully 50–60% of shares outstanding are often owned by institutional investors who have some angle on SRI, whereas if your company is headquartered in the US, this percentage has been closer to 15%.[22] This disparity is starting to change, as corporates in the US have become increasingly interested in sustainability as a driver of future outperformance and differentiation. If you are based in Australia where drought and other climate extremes have been recently prevalent, these issues are now seen as strictly business critical. In Asia, nothing could be clearer than the fact that three things are essential to success as companies attempt to emerge as global players: 1) establishing trust in your brand, 2) overcoming pollution risks and 3) seizing related environmental opportunities, such as scaling cheap solar as the cost curves continue to change, which would also benefit from renewed global regulation and financial support from governments. In many ways, countries like China and the companies within will succeed or fail strictly on the basis of trust, as well as through building global bridges and avoiding unnecessary tariff wars in the process.

Call this sustainability or not – either way, these are now factors of critical import to potential business success overall, and the field of SRI needs to drop the terminology war and simply ensure that values and value-seeking are aligned and maximized. Assets deployed in the fashion described in this chapter remain niche, but are the growing segment of

SRI. All of this is part of the global shift we see happening, which can be summarized in the next chapter as the evolution of SRI continues into ESG integration and beyond.

....

CHAPTER 4

Megatrends in Sustainable Investing

The systemic nature of global equity ownership

RECENT META-ANALYSIS AT NSFM, derived from parsing through a myriad of industry sources, demonstrates the diffuse nature of global equity ownership as it stands today (see Figure 1).

FIGURE 1. Global equity ownership by asset owner category (in %).

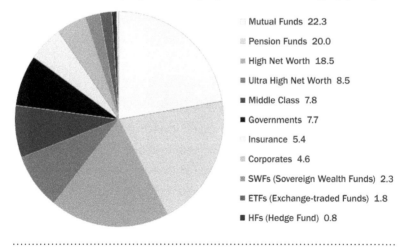

Mutual Funds 22.3

Pension Funds 20.0

High Net Worth 18.5

Ultra High Net Worth 8.5

Middle Class 7.8

Governments 7.7

Insurance 5.4

Corporates 4.6

SWFs (Sovereign Wealth Funds) 2.3

ETFs (Exchange-traded Funds) 1.8

HFs (Hedge Fund) 0.8

With global public equity representing approximately US$65T in market value, global mutual funds represent the largest category of ownership at 22.5% (and note that over half of mutual fund ownership comes from the US). Pension funds on a global basis have been shrinking somewhat but still own 20%, with a growing percentage of this segment being increasingly passively managed. High net worth, and the rapidly growing segment of ultra high net worth (typically defined as owning over $30M in assets) combined, now represents 27%, the highest segment of all if counted as one category, and the remaining segments another 30.5%. Clearly, any changes to the status quo will be challenging given the systemically diffuse nature of ownership.

Additional categories include (in descending order) middle-class individual investors in aggregate, government stakes in companies, companies owning stakes in other companies, sovereign wealth funds, hedge funds, exchange traded funds (these last three categories having grown over the last decade or more) and lastly, endowments and foundations in aggregate, which own roughly 0.3% of global public equity.

Global sustainable investing in practice

A report by the Global Sustainable Investment Alliance (**www.gsi-alliance.org**, a consortium involving lead members ASrIA, Eurosif, RIAA, SIO, UKSIF, US SIF and VBDO in the Netherlands) recently claimed that US$13.6T of equity is managed by investors looking at sustainability.

However, after a full review, NSFM found this number to be closer to US$1.5T at most, almost a tenth of the claim above. This figure represents less than 5% of the US$32T managed by signatories to the UN Principles for Responsible Investment and approximately 1% of global assets under management overall.

Much, if not all, of the US$11.1T in the gap between the GSIA findings and ours are large pension funds that engage with companies and otherwise invest in benchmark indices or through external managers. Additional large elements of this $11.1T gap would include large asset owners who deploy a single sector screen, say on tobacco or business activity in Sudan, or have divested from a very small number of select companies.

On a regional basis, in the US we see at most $100B in managed portfolios applying ESG factors actively. Much of the $1.5T we see is in Europe. Dutch pension fund PGGM, for example, screens out bottom performers by sector, and otherwise does not apply ESG to its holdings, so should all of their equity be included? Right now it is in our $1.5T figure (hence this figure could be even smaller, if you believe that company positions that survive such a first screen are otherwise not affected further by ESG analysis).

....

FIGURE 2. Global sustainable equity portfolios by region.

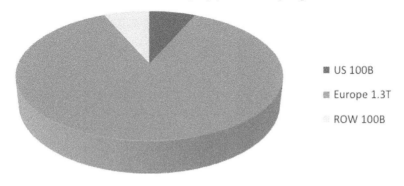

- US 100B
- Europe 1.3T
- ROW 100B

....

We also see a further $1T of investment likely to begin factoring in ESG or sustainability considerations over the next one to two years. Norges Bank, for example, while divested from a small handful of companies at present, and engaging on governance issues, is in the early days of developing investment strategies along the three themes they have identified as most substantial: climate change, water and children.

In the US, CalPERS also have recently announced a Sustainable Investing Research Initiative which may result in conclusions on sustainability factors that would start to affect their investment decisions. Presently, however, both Norges Bank and CalPERS are largely invested in the status quo, and so they do not get significantly added to our figures on presently invested assets making active or passive decisions on ESG factors.

Looking to the future, an important, potentially increasing, bridge between global corporates, fund managers and asset owners can be seen, together seeking deeply embedded sustainability. We also take heart in the growing recognition that asset-owner collaboration at scale on these issues has the potential to start moving companies to improve their performance in a race for capital. But it will likely require collaboration across asset-owner groups including not only pension funds, but also the very wealthiest individuals and families around the world to achieve a meaningful consensus.

We see a further breakdown in this $1.5T emerging between negative and positive strategies, with only $400B in funds seeking to find best performers by sector or in general from sustainability factors.

With only $1.5T presently invested in global public equity portfolios through sustainable, responsible, ethical or whatever terminology you choose, this could be seen as a call to do nothing by corporates and governments if the interest is not there. There is great urgency to drive the sort of change that sustainable investors seek, but the present state of affairs is not working to affect that change, and so it is of the most vital importance to recognize this and figure out what we need instead to bring about the changes we seek (and likely require) for the sake of our survival, resilience, health and economic well-being.

SRI, ESG and beyond

The two well-worn three letter acronyms, SRI and ESG, in effect describe the transition from First Wave SRI and its negative roots, towards a more data-driven review of ESG factors. The ESG data being reviewed and utilized, however, are still to this day all too often retrospective and negative, looking at aspects such as human rights violations, environmental spills, governance failures, etc. All such ESG factors are potentially important and material, but they can fail to capture the positive trends and categories of opportunity that are emerging. Hence, the Parnassus approach appeals, designed as it is to capture companies as they emerge from ESG problems into becoming either better performers or solution providers. Their Black Hills case study on the subject is also worth a read through in this regard.[23]

Overall, however, there remains a significant gap between most modern-day investment strategies and environmental reality, and something will have to give at some point soon. The gap between ownership and environmental risk remains one of many areas of difference between mainstream financial services institutions and those that increasing emphasis on environmental, social and governance factors.

With all of this in mind, three other trends are important to consider, perhaps above and beyond ESG, as follows:

1. Automation

Automation continues to change the playing field, as companies look to maximize their profit through efficiencies. Innovation also emerges as a key driver of both growth and productivity, as well as a way to provide well-being within potential environmental and resource constraints. The importance of technology, automation and innovation has led to the tech sector becoming the largest component of the S&P 500, as well as the continued outperformance of the Nasdaq 100 companies. Automation is also a challenge for society and the economy, as demands on company efficiency means workers are at times left to the side if they cannot keep up. Aside from the societal cost, as business as a whole learns to be productive with fewer workers per product produced, the economy needs to find a way to create more jobs to pick up the slack, or unemployment will be a drag on corporate returns.

2. Globalization

In the search for efficiency, the West continues to rapidly outsource functions to low cost centers. Bangladesh may be the lowest cost center of all, as became evident from the recent horrific factory fire, where multiple Wal-Mart suppliers clearly stretched the limits of worker safety and conditions too far. Supply chains have become more visible and it is expected that demands for transparency will increase pressure on companies to raise their game and behave more fairly towards workers. You can now see the top tier of any large company's suppliers on a

Bloomberg terminal. Puma has demonstrated that any company can achieve a comprehensive perspective on all tiers of their supply chain, all the way to the raw materials level. Transparency is one thing: the bigger question is what to do about the problems it reveals, and to move towards creating more prosperity and avoiding potential environmental tipping points and categories of resource constraint.

Globalization is also slowly moving us to global fairness, and this too is a good thing, but not always something well recognized by investors. As companies outsource more functions while seeking efficiency, developing economies improve, and the playing field continues to level. Given that the larger problems we face are global in nature, we would benefit from this level playing field, even though there will be cost as we adjust to this balancing trend. Investors would be wise to anticipate this global transition, as they consider not only asset allocation percentages but regional ones as well. Most investors continue to deploy weightings most heavily to their local regions, but it would seem wise to take a global perspective now and anticipate the field continuing to level out. Technology is making Africa more competitive for example, with cellphones empowering entrepreneurship. Local problems manifest differently, however, including how climate change will affect regions. Remaining resources also are a major economic factor and will continue to be, for example, pressures on fresh water in China, dwindling phosphorus resources now largely in Morocco, tar sands in Canada, coal moving from Australia to China, etc. A third important trend category is thus regionality.

3. Regionality

While globalization continues its inexorable march forward, the regional differences that manifest are emerging as equally, if not more, important, including the local and community opportunities that continue to excite and emerge from the world of impact investing.

The failed climate negotiations of the UN are proof of the challenges that remain from taking a region versus region approach to global issues. As witnessed in Doha in 2012, pitting one region against another without an agenda, and requiring unanimous consent, is a futile task, and one which the UN would be wise to consider abolishing.

A different perspective starts to emerge if you look at the three AGR (automation, globalization, regionality) factors above as categories of opportunity, especially with a sustainability lens applied.

Automation, technology and innovation are means by which companies can improve their operations and profit. Identifying winners from that perspective would seem wise to at least consider. If you don't think of Apple as a company in this category, one that has greatly lowered the cost and footprint of computing when you consider the much lower cost of powering an iPhone5 versus a desktop computer, then you simply aren't paying attention. While it might have been difficult to spot this when Apple was suffering at $10 a share 12–15 years ago, before Steve Jobs's return, it was certainly clearly in view when I first taught a class on Sustainability & Investing at Columbia's Earth Institute in 2009, with Apple trading for roughly $190 a share.[24] Some ESG data providers may disagree with this assessment and here in many ways is where the rubber meets the road on Values versus Value Investing. We have seen Apple appear at the bottom of some ESG lists when it comes to past issues, but in fairness they have been keenly focused on performing social audits of their facilities in China, for example, for some time now. Understanding companies and going beyond publicly available information is critical to getting ESG right as a filter.

The even bigger, and still largely untapped, opportunity here is for companies to identify revenue from sustainability driven innovation. GE has arguably benefited greatly from this approach through its ecomagination platform, without which its share price may well have suffered further during the financial crisis. Other companies such as Dow have also made good strides in this area, but much work remains, and identifying companies that can exceed future revenue estimates due to sustainability opportunity will be an area to watch very closely indeed.

In some ways, the most positive opportunity among AGR would be the regional aspect, especially within the framework of so-called impact investing. A somewhat nebulous and confusing concept at times, an impact investment can be best explained as an investment that has a local or community benefit, an environmental benefit, as well as a financial benefit. Some confuse impact investing with the entire field of SRI, but the common denominator across true impact investing is that it has a local focus on a specific community. Focusing on how to help local communities flourish can include ways of ensuring sustainability across agriculture, fresh water, or energy from wind or solar. Such investments can also help reduce transportation costs and impacts, while helping focus and fix societal problems and challenges very specifically with targeted investment pools of capital. It is early days for this area of work, though it is a framework of great interest and seems to be starting to emerge as a solution especially in parts of Asia. Imagine a scenario where Chinese communities were strengthened through implementation of impact investing before the US takes it to scale? There is potential for an Impact Race, much as the Space Race got us to the Moon (but only after seeing the Soviets take it to heart first).

....

CHAPTER 5

Scenarios and Pathways: Implications for Investors

THERE WOULD APPEAR TO BE three prospective response scenarios on issues of the environment and society for investors to consider. The first 'option', business as usual, is where most investors are presently placed, leading to some form or other of catastrophe whether related to storms, biodiversity loss, sea level rise, etc., or some combination thereof, and very likely economic collapse. A second overarching scenario, incremental change, on the other hand appears to be insufficient. We struggle to find adequate pathways to sustainability through 'wedge' theory. The latest estimates across analysis ranging from the International Energy Agency's future studies and similar from the International Finance Corporation (IFC), World Resources Institute (WRI) and UN Environment Programme (UNEP) suggest we are on the brink of big trouble with incremental approaches being anything but close to enough.

If the possible outcomes are either radical transformation or catastrophe, this has enormous implications for investors. A point to stress is that it should be clear that if investors stand pat, they will fail either way. Therefore, the only sensible choice is for fund managers and asset owners to change their priorities and perspectives and seek to become part of the solution instead of participating in an almost guaranteed economic or environmental failure over time.

The state of global ownership

The present state of global asset owners requires some consideration. Pension funds, endowments and foundations typically have ongoing shortfalls, paying out more on an annual basis than they earn in profit. Such pools of assets feel the need to use a mix of creative expectation to maintain as much of their own status quo as they possibly can. Pension funds often report profit expectations of 5–8% per year in an age where growth is fundamentally challenged. Yet these same asset owners insist on being universal owners, not factoring in ESG in any meaningful way, perhaps guaranteeing that they won't achieve their own goals if growth fails to continue. Fortunately, as we saw in the previous chapter many large asset owners are reconsidering this, including CalPERS, Norges Bank and many others, especially those in Scandinavia. Such asset owners represent well over $1T in public equity alone, making a pending shift of this capital towards sustainability focused companies another trend to consider.

Another aspect to discuss more thoroughly is the deeply rooted nature of current lifestyles and business. The global footprint in effect consists mostly of individuals and their families, businesses, governments, and the business processes, transportation and buildings involved. Entrenched deeply within all aspects of this are use of fossil fuels, cement and chemicals, all of which are the vast majority of the overall greenhouse gas (GHG) footprint of human activity. Businesses encompass roughly 40% of the global footprint, individuals another 40–50%, and natural causes are the remainder.[25] PwC suggests that we need to lower the aggregate annual footprint by 5% per year, in order to keep within a 2°C increase by the year 2050.[26] Clearly, business has a huge role here, in promoting and delivering resource efficiency and innovative products and solutions which can further reduce individual footprints. Using investment to encourage such activity, by rewarding those companies best positioned to drive solutions of the future, is worth a concerted effort, and to some degree, markets are already moving in that direction. In 2011, for example, while the S&P 500 was flat, two leading lists of the most innovative US companies, one performed by MIT Sloan, the other by 'strategy + business' magazine, were both up +6%.

> If outperformance can come from companies that are most innovative in finding sustainability solutions, while keeping an eye on their bottom lines, we may well have the strategy we require right there – Buy Right and Hold. If a large enough tranche of investors weighted companies best positioned in this regard, and further made clear that to gain investment, companies needed to move in this direction post haste, we would really have something useful to consider for all stakeholders.

One other thing worth considering is the overall ownership structure of business. The largest categories of owners of stocks are governments, wealthy families and individuals, corporations themselves, pension funds, sovereign wealth funds, insurance companies and middle-class families in aggregate. Much smaller in aggregate are endowments and foundations, less than 1% of public equity in total, so efforts at getting universities to divest from fossil fuels, while perhaps morally feel good in nature, will not tip the balance in any way shape or form. (More interesting are cases such as Yale University's endowment, who already allocated 6.4% of their ownership to 'positive sustainable investment'.[27] However, does this imply that 93.6% of their investing is not sustainable? Perhaps not all of it, but it does beg the question. Certainly universities have the opportunity to set an example, but they cannot do it all by themselves.)

Long-term energy transitions are required

So what sort of larger shifts are required to get us to 2050 without climate catastrophe? One thing we could consider starting with is coal. Can we not consider a preservation and buyout effort to retire those assets in the ground, combined with converting coal plants to use other sources? Some form of effort in this regard would seem mandatory. While the Obama administration is embarking on technical policies making coal plants unaffordable, Europe is slipping back into increased coal use, especially after Fukushima. China, Russia and India in the meantime continue to make plans to create well over a thousand new coal plants. Coal represents a large majority of the problem, and if we found a way to completely convert coal plants to natural gas using best practice to ensure no methane leakage and limit the damage to fresh water in the process by choosing locations wisely, we could have something of a plan to pursue. Ownership is critical, as assets in the ground have an assumed value. Much like bankruptcy proceedings, owners of equity and fixed income that relate to coal companies could receive some percentage of their investment back, and owners of the land, whether the same companies or not, could simply be bought out, and a regime put in place to ensure that the coal stays where it is, in the ground. Similar efforts are deployed on aging nuclear weapons and nuclear waste, making sure they don't leak, proliferate, etc. This comes at a cost, but one we have to bear. Investors should get part of their money back, but not all, as there need to be penalties for choices taken that prove in the end to be economically unwise. Why should investors get a free pass? They seek one, but it is not deserved in this case.

Nuclear makes some sense as a viable option – certainly France has shown how nuclear can be a majority of the energy source for a country. Can France lead a global coalition to deploy best practice nuclear? The challenge of course is that the best technologies are more expensive, and it takes something like 20 years to deploy nuclear, especially in the US, while Fukushima has derailed options elsewhere, and the waste challenge remains.

Clearly, we also need to find a way to maximize solar, wind, hydro, geothermal, etc. The good news here is that the technologies improve every day, along something of a Moore's Law/Kurzweilian path. The bad news is that these same advances have caused early investors to lose their shirts and at times give up on environmental investing as a viable option. This is one of the reasons to map out a transition plan that investors can ride with confidence, and not just invest where their hearts are.

Oil is the big gorilla in some ways. Oil use is baked in to our infrastructure to a very large degree. Families own cars with requisite lifestyles not easily replaced. Businesses and their supply chains rely heavily on petroleum use. It is not likely that this can be easily transitioned in a dramatic way, and so the answer here may be to do what we can radically on coal, harness gas safely and maximize oil use efficiencies in the short term. In the longer term we need to transition away from petroleum as well, but we need to get started, and solutions here will also evolve in the next 5 to 10 years. This is also why demonizing the oil companies is not the answer. Oil companies are simply companies – in 5 to 10 years some of them may diversify into other sources of energy, and so they can be encouraged to be part of the answer. First and foremost, they should be required to refrain from enabling what have been successful and very damaging disinformation campaigns. If investors achieved only this, it would be a significant achievement worth vigorous pursuit.

Further to pathways to 2050, when you look at the International Energy Agency (IEA) and Shell scenarios alongside the Carbon Tracker Initiative's findings, a macro-path starts to emerge. Carbon Tracker has found that we can burn only so much more carbon and stay within some confidence of climate safety. The cost of catastrophe would be very high as Hurricane Sandy taught us recently. In effect, as of 2013, we can likely only burn a further 500 gigatons (Gt) of carbon dioxide. Yet we've burned roughly 65 Gt in the last two years, so time is running out rapidly. Assuming the remaining 500 Gt total is the limit for 2013–2050, then, Table 1 offers a pathway which could work.

TABLE 1. Emissions scenario for a sustainable world

2013–2020	200 Gt (21 + 3.9/yr as opposed to 28.2 + 3.9)
2021–2030	150 Gt (12.5 + 2.5/yr)
2031–2040	100 Gt (10 + 0/yr)
2041–2050	50 Gt (5 + 0/yr)

We need to start at once moving from 30+ Gt/year burning of GHGs to 20–25 Gt/year, on average, by 2020. Each year we delay, the effort required increases. This is accomplishable through parallel efforts to migrate away from coal, increasing use of technology, changing mileage minimums on cars, increasing renewables, etc. 2021 through 2030 then needs to see a further push down to an average of 12.5 Gt/year, in combination with restorative efforts that can reduce land use impacts and related factors. In 2031 through 2040, further restorative movement and efficiencies could bring us to 10 Gt/year, and down to 5Gt/year by the following decade, and then we have something of a plan that could actually work.

We really would benefit from mapping business as usual benchmarks to a transition plan like this, and start to get passive owners of scale such as pension funds to invest accordingly. This would force business to move with the plan, or be left behind in a chase for diminishing capital. More work is needed on this transition agenda, but we can at least encourage with investment the sort of changes we require.

What this scale of transition would require has serious implications for sectors including utilities, oil, water, agriculture, and of course all the sectors indirectly using these commodities and resources. What sector weightings should look like in this regard in future is not necessarily relevant now in 2013, but will be when transition needs to occur. If we could use 2013 and 2014 to figure this out, in 2015 we could start to massively implement changes, and move capital on a global basis, with agreed carbon constraints, whether through taxes or otherwise, to create the necessary economic incentives that would in effect force the corporate mass to reconfigure into the organizations we require for a sustainable world.

An economic roadmap to a sustainable 2050

What sort of reweighting does this start to look like? For one, utilities need to transition perhaps the most: electricity generation from coal is the highest percentage of the global footprint, and much of the coal is transported across country. Tariffs could actually become a mechanism – for example, coal from Australia to China has the highest embedded water of any flow of resources globally. Calculating the flows and use patterns against the sort of energy use we require, can start to show where the problems are. Incentivizing energy production and maximizing efficiencies on a local basis also makes a great deal of sense. Different regions will require varying techniques and implementations. There likely needs to be some price on carbon in some fashion to get the ball rolling. Utilities can help transition to more local generation and much is already happening in this respect. Utilities need to either become part of the answer, or we need alternative solutions – in some ways it is that simple, and capital is what helps them facilitate the status quo. Investors need to coalesce on a utilities transition plan, and engage corporates and governments for the changes we all require, exactly what capital deployment can make happen.

There are implications for all industries – the automotive sector is seeing this, and trying to plan for the future, and they need to be encouraged to innovate and to experiment. Capital can help. Agriculture sees this, and is desperate to find ways to use resources more efficiently. The beverage industry is deeply involved in water challenges. Mainstream investors need to see what's already happening, and not just ride out unsupportable business models. Asset allocation changes can also help.

Infrastructure, fixed income and private equity professionals are all seeing the need to take these matters seriously. Community and local investing, what I earlier called 'impact investing', could also help drive changes in the manner outlined above. Microcredit, microfinance and other creative means of financing have all been exciting developments, but unless scalable in a meaningful way along the sorts of macro-numbers above, they won't be an important part of the answer, so finding mechanisms to make that happen remain an important challenge.

Can we start benchmarking asset owners on all of the above? Are they on the roadmap or not, and can grassroots pressure be brought to asset owners on a global scale to press them to get on this transition plan and stick with it? That would be an essential place to start.

One key scenario to consider is the work of Amory Lovins, especially his roadmap to 2050 in the book *Reinventing Fire* (Chelsea Green, 2012). He sees a combination of approaches leading to successful navigation of the otherwise perilous path we face through an energy future that uses a combination of natural gas, renewables, efficiency and more, in combination with weaning ourselves off coal and oil completely. Playing this scenario out across our current sectors, mapping what needs to occur over time, and you start to see a roadmap unfurl for investors to participate in at scale. This would ensure the transition is encouraged. Investment institutions should be reporting their progress on this basis, or be held to account, so that the overall systemic trend is maintained. Failure to achieve some form of systemic shift of this nature is too onerous a risk to consider, and so we need to start planning for a 'checks and balances' system of reporting and investment that ensures companies in aggregate move us to where we need to go. If business knew this sort of regime were coming, getting in front of this trend in the short term would create its own positive dynamic, and further sort out winners and losers accordingly.

The IEA, Shell and BP also publish future scenarios work that is worth a look, but as you might imagine the oil companies don't have as radical a view on oil, funnily (or not) enough. The IEA work on the future of the Nordic region is of particular interest.[28] If each region had a plan to evolve into maximizing renewables and efficiency along similar lines to the Nordic region, and follow a carbon-neutral energy path to 2050, we'd start to have roadmaps showing a way forward, perhaps in combination with some form of transition plan for investors to use as a new benchmark. Investors, recall, own something like 70% of public companies, and quite a share of private companies as well. Governments own a large percentage of enterprises as well. Investors and governments aligned and committed to invest in a sustainable future is without question the sort of systemic change we require.

....

CHAPTER 6
ESG Factor Specifics and Other Trends to Consider

LET'S TAKE A BRIEF STEP BACK now that we are considering some of the larger issues that will be facing us in the coming decades, with a look a bit more broadly at ESG factors.

Social and governance factors abound and need careful consideration. However, we also need to caution against a blah, grey application of ESG past performances more broadly as anything but misguided. In this age of transparency, companies like Apple publish lists of their suppliers. Bloomberg terminals now carry lists of the largest suppliers and customers of the biggest publicly traded companies. What this means from a social perspective is that human rights, labor and other related issues, while important, are harder abuses to get away with, and it will only get more difficult to do so as transparency increases globally. That's a good thing, but it also means that tilting a large cap portfolio towards best social actors isn't easily done. Few if any large cap companies with a public presence can afford to get these things wrong. And so criteria are important, but not investible in any meaningful way, even while a majority of socially responsible (SRI) assets are deployed primarily on this basis.

The discrepancy between where SRI assets are deployed vs where the most material risks truly reside helps explain why mainstream investors don't give ESG factors due consideration.

Corporate governance is another minefield. Globally, countries such as Germany thrive regardless of the US model of governance of discouraging board conflicts, which the German/Japanese model discards. The bottom line is that one must now parse through ESG factors between those that are most material versus those that are risks to keep in mind, but which may well not ever manifest in a meaningful way, or at minimum, can be navigated successfully by companies. But it is useful to consider ESG factors overall in some fashion to see what all of the issues are in one go.

The most simple, powerful statement I've seen of what is most important, can be summed up by a review of the United Nations Global Compact (UNGC) and their Ten Principles. The UNGC asks companies to embrace, support and enact, within their sphere of influence, a set of core values in the areas of human rights, labor standards, the environment and anti-corruption:

....

TABLE 2. The Ten Principles of the United Nations Global Compact[29]
....
Human rights
....
Principle 1: Businesses should support and respect the protection of internationally proclaimed human rights; and
....
Principle 2: make sure that they are not complicit in human rights abuses.
....

Labor

Principle 3: Businesses should uphold the freedom of association and the effective recognition of the right to collective bargaining;

Principle 4: the elimination of all forms of forced and compulsory labor;

Principle 5: the effective abolition of child labor; and

Principle 6: the elimination of discrimination in respect of employment and occupation.

Environment

Principle 7: Businesses should support a precautionary approach to environmental challenges;

Principle 8: undertake initiatives to promote greater environmental responsibility; and

Principle 9: encourage the development and diffusion of environmentally friendly technologies.

Anti-corruption

Principle 10: Businesses should work against corruption in all its forms, including extortion and bribery.

These are 10 honorable and somewhat all-encompassing principles, but enforcement at scale isn't available, so companies can join the Global Compact and file an unaudited report, but little gets accomplished, which is frustrating. But imagine the impact of global mandatory auditable disclosure on these Ten Principles, so they stand as a reasonable framework of potentially material ESG impacts against which corporates and investors measure themselves.

Also important to consider are a number of other emerging trends across sustainability reporting and standard setting and one can start to see how parallel efforts could help lead to positive change, even in the absence of some form of global mandatory auditable disclosure.

The evolving integrated reporting efforts are perhaps most interesting to consider. The concept here is that companies should issue a single report, combining both financial and sustainability criteria, and the commonality is the strategy that overlaps both. The Prince of Wales has taken a keen interest in, and helps oversee, the International Integrated Reporting Council (IIRC), which recently launched a very impressive Prototype Framework,[30] just accepted and in public comment mode at the time of writing. This represents a major step forward in providing a clear path to reporting that puts company performance in context. The idea of sustainability context and thresholds continues to be championed by Vermont's Mark McElroy and Bill Baue, as a further example, whereby 'tipping points' on carbon emissions and other environmental factors are specifically built in to portfolios and corporate target considerations.[31]

Standards are perhaps shockingly still largely lacking, although the GHG Protocol has coalesced and been accepted as a way of describing the footprint of an organization. Thus, Scope 1 represents the direct operations and services provided, Scope 2 the purchased electricity, and Scope 3 the indirect footprint. Scope 3 has two parts in effect: upstream effects, which are the elements purchased for companies to create their products and services, and downstream effects of the products in use. This framework applies not only to public and private companies, but any organization, and it can be used not only on environmental impacts, but social and governance concerns as well.

Beyond this, an effort deserving close attention is the Sustainability Accounting Standards Board (SASB). This effort is looking at one industry at a time, and setting key performance indicators (KPIs) for materiality by sector for use by investors, and in regulatory filings. This effort will be an important one, especially if they provide context and scenarios as apparently planned. SASB is an open process, and involvement is encouraged – see more at **www.sasb.org**.

Other efforts worth watching include the Global Reporting Initiative (GRI), which is currently on version 3.1 and is now moving to 4.0 – although why frameworks of this nature need to keep evolving is an important question. I find GRI 3.1 to be a very useful taxonomy of ESG issues, but not all appear to be material, while others are very material but somewhat vaguely stated, and GRI has not dealt with the context issue, which remains a concern, even as they pursue 4.0. However, this reporting framework has gained important traction, and is useful to review for those looking at what sort of granular ESG issues are potentially worthy of consideration. The letter grade approach of GRI is admirable, but again, as it relies on voluntary reporting, a partial database is only ever available – see more at **www.globalreporting.org**.

Some combination of SASB, Integrated Reporting, GRI, the GHG Protocol and similar efforts starts to provide an overarching framework of ESG criteria, but the field has not coalesced by any means. This is why there remains a plethora of data providers in the ESG space, and they can all carve out something of a reasonable niche with varying frameworks, priorities and specific perspectives.

ESG data on global companies, however, is not robust in any meaningful way. For example, developing world company data largely remain lacking

– especially countries such as China and Russia – meaning that investors, never having a full and trustworthy dataset on these issues, cannot invest in confidence around ESG subjects comprehensively. Some form of the previously mentioned global mandatory auditable disclosure would help, however, there is no global body to enforce and regulate something like this. The United Nations is not this body, and it remains a challenge to figure out what this should look like, and how to bring it to fruition.

Lacking this framework for comprehensive data, providers use emerging guidelines and standards, and are building data as we speak, even if it is partial by definition. Those providers include longstanding MSCI, who rolled together former providers KLD, Innovest and Riskmetrics. Sustainalytics is an up-and-comer worth a close watch as they encourage the development of quality employees, a recipe for success in any business. EIRIS is a longstanding ESG data provider that has garnered trust, and Bloomberg emerges as the sole mainstream organization building ESG data themselves. Bloomberg's commitment is tangible – one wishes they would fully integrate ESG considerations into their radio and TV franchises as well, but they are a key driver, funding SASB and even the Sierra Club's efforts to move beyond coal, so they are always one to watch, especially as Michael Bloomberg reaches the end of his term as Mayor of New York City. He has seen via Hurricane Sandy the urgency that is now clearly required. There are other niche players to mention as well. Trucost on the environmental impacts side provides the best comprehensive, global perspective of environmental impacts, perhaps best seen in the *Newsweek* Green Rankings that places US and global companies into perspective, combined with Sustainalytics and their qualitative view, and whose data are publicly available at **www. newsweek.com/green**. A fascinating 'public perception vs reality' study was performed in 2012 by *Newsweek* for the first time which was largely overlooked, and is also worth examining **http://www.thedailybeast.com/ newsweek/2012/10/22/newsweek-green-rankings-2012-results-of-the- green-brands-survey.html**. GMI Ratings is the global leader on corporate governance, especially the US model as championed by thought-leader Robert A.G. Monks, whose recent books are extremely relevant to the challenges we are discussing, especially on the issues of ownership and control (see his *Citizens DisUnited*, Miniver Press, 2013). Other more niche players exist globally, and it has been long suspected further consolidation will occur in this space. Fund managers also have seen pressure on their levels of profit, and in the UK alone a number of longstanding players have been scaling down or outsourcing their operations, including Henderson Global Investors, Aviva and F&C.

Moving beyond niche approaches

What this confirms to me is that the SRI/ESG spaces as practiced are niche. These matters should not be niche, in fact it is an imperative that they are not so, but they will continue to be until the materiality of sustainability is robustly defined. The opportunity remains for corporates to specifically spell out the future revenue they seek from sustainability strategies and initiatives, as well as that revenue which is specifically at risk. Short, medium and long term, we need to see corporates demonstrating this understanding, as well as developing and encouraging the sense that more regulation is required to move us along the previously described transition plan and avoid the dangerous terrain we otherwise face.

Ask any family, interested in their own protection and well-being, and if there is something absolutely guaranteed to affect their lives in a negative way on the horizon, whether they would want something done about it or not? They would all answer in the affirmative without question. Ask investors the same thing about the financial health of their portfolios: if they knew something was going to affect them negatively and was on the relatively immediate horizon, would they take steps of some kind? Perhaps a hedging strategy, asset reallocation, investigation of winners and losers around the key emerging issue, etc.? Investors do this sort of thing all the time when they perceive that a particular topic looks likely to have financial ramifications to the value of the stakes they own in companies and their issued securities.

Regardless of these familial and investor instincts, we have at hand issues of dire magnitude to families, businesses and portfolios which are being largely ignored, and they are coming directly from the realm of ESG, but ESG practice has confused almost everyone as to what is really important. Everyone has their own way of prioritizing such factors, whereby one of E, S or G becomes what really motivates, with the other two being secondary. As a result, ESG is really six acronyms, depending on the fund or industry practitioner, and so you really have each of ESG, EGS, SGE, SEG, GSE and GES. Few in the industry would admit to this, and the 'all or nothing' implication of ESG, combined with a lack of portfolio outperformance over time, has likely limited mainstream take-up of these issues to some degree.
....

CHAPTER 7

Steps to Consider in Constructing a Sustainable Portfolio

Universe

WITH ANY ATTEMPT TO BUILD A PORTFOLIO, sustainable or otherwise, first a *potential* universe needs to be chosen. Public equity is by far the largest component of global investment, worth roughly 20 times all privately held enterprises combined. So, for the sake of this conversation, we are focusing on public equity, but other asset owners may also want to apply sustainability constructs to their holdings in other asset classes such as fixed income, private equity, infrastructure, real estate and commodities.

Sustainability issues are global, and so therefore should be the universe of companies considered in a sustainable portfolio. Some have tried to design sustainable portfolios by country or region, but this always feels incomplete. What if the opportunities first emerge elsewhere in an age of globalization? Most successful sustainability-focused fund managers have not made regional distinctions, and so we will not either.

Of the major index providers, MSCI appears to have emerged with by far the most global traction, and so we suggest MSCI World[32] as a good benchmark to compare any resulting portfolio against. However, MSCI World represents only 'developed' world countries, and so in addition we will suggest the

MSCI Emerging Markets Index,[33] even as the MSCI World seems to be a reasonable comparison for future performance. Between these developed and developing world indexes there are over 4000 companies to choose from: a challenging number to cover. However, there are no shortcuts to finding the best opportunities, and so one should be diligent and thorough, especially if sustainability is to drive future outperformance. The next step then is to determine an approach to whittling down this universe, and thus we need to consider sector allocations.

Weightings and other construction issues

The first thing to suggest beyond focusing on a global universe is that whatever the end number of securities owned – and 50–100 seems a reasonable number – the holdings should be equally weighted. Research shows that equal weighting is a good approach for any strategy, and I will refer you to the excellent *Successful Investing is a Process* (Wiley, 2013) by Jacques Lussier for more information. So, let us assume that we will hold anywhere from 100 stocks with 1% of our investment in each company down to 50 companies at 2% per investment. The next step is determining sector and regional allocations.

As you can see here at **http://seekingalpha.com/article/320168-s-p-500-historical-sector-weightings**, the S&P 500 has had varying sector percentages of value over time, and these hold true globally as well. A discussion of a few of these sectors is in order.

Technology companies are a natural for a future oriented portfolio for many reasons. Such companies will provide efficiency solutions (IBM and SAP both make a business out of sustainability; Apple has arguably lowered the environmental footprint of doing business through cloud computing and has targeted meeting 100% of its energy demand through renewable sources). We suggest at least a double weighting in technology.

Financial services have been challenged. This sector has failed on key metrics of sustainability including trust and transparency, and fails to take the sustainability opportunity seriously for the most part. We will half weight this sector. These two approaches alone would have resulted in much outperformance over the last five years.

Energy is a challenging sector. There is not been much recent out-performance versus broader index investing (though there was 5 to 10 years ago), and oil and gas companies face future challenges not only on environmental concerns, but also from a supply and demand perspective. We think a rational response to this sector – which is likely to remain under a variety of pressures – is half weighting. Arguably some companies in this space may emerge with important solutions and the infrastructure to drive needed change, so keeping a close eye is required. Companies such as Chevron, ExxonMobil, BP and Shell also have many challenges in managing ongoing global spills, cleanups, reputational challenges, again all price pressure considerations. Other sectors require a careful eye to ensure that they aren't being driven down by globalization or automation pressures. But for the sake of this exercise, let's keep weights level on all other sectors. Utilities is an interesting one to watch, as consumers demand low prices, while the cost curves keep changing on the available energy mix and infrastructure builds of the future are likely to rely on natural gas which if cheaper than coal, will be a positive step (but only if regulated properly). There is also much momentum behind local sourcing of future energy. So we will keep a level weight on this sector, but this too may be a sector of future concern. Looking at smaller industries, the pressures are all too clear on publishing, education, and even telecommunications, which may be affected by increasing innovation through technology and the internet.

Examples of how a sector focus can affect investing: over the last five years, the S&P 500 was +15%, while the Vanguard Financials ETF was -22% and the Vanguard Energy ETF nearly flat, while the Nasdaq 100 was ahead approximately 50%. A sector focus on one's equity investing alone would have yielded great recent results.

As we enter a new paradigm, underweighting sectors under pressure emerges as sound strategy for consideration (but watch undervaluation carefully to not miss market runs) while overweighting others which figure to drive the changes we seek.

With all this in mind, one can start to see a portfolio emerge, but we need a clear set of criteria for choosing specific companies to invest in.

Choosing companies

Most portfolios have one overarching theme. Either they are focused on finding great value from a bottom-up analysis approach, or focus on top-down allocations, or similar. We are focused on finding the sustainability opportunities of tomorrow, while avoiding overvaluation. This mandates the following approach across five factors:

a. find companies most willing to innovate and drive solutions that can change the systemic problems we face most urgently;

b. find companies with the culture and individuals at the top who are committed to this sort of change and approach;

c. find companies who are willing to do so with a business model in mind to ensure ongoing success, ideally measuring and reporting on their revenue from sustainable products in the process;

d. find companies with the cash in hand to invest in the business opportunities of tomorrow and those who can scale such innovations to market most successfully; and

e. find companies not burdened by legacy problems that can get in the way of their success in this regard.

A close examination of the over 4000 companies in the MSCI World and Emerging Markets indices may well not find any company who gets a perfect score on these five categories. However, one can locate companies who are heading in a better direction in these respects, and otherwise do not outright fail in any of them.

GE, for example, has shown a willingness to innovate, has a growing percentage of revenue coming from its 'ecomagination' segment, and is among the global companies with the most cash in hand. GE is in many ways burdened by its diversification into financial services, without which it would arguably be worth much more, and so there is another opportunity here – investing ahead of a scenario where GE diversifies out of financial services.

Apple, as previously outlined, is focused strongly on its environmental and social risks and opportunities. The main question with Apple is whether its share price has gotten ahead of its true value. We first identified Apple as a good investment in 2009 when its share price was $190, which would have been a good time to get in. At this point, there is a question as to how much more product innovation it can drive versus the price it already trades at today (mid $400s or thereabout).

We aren't going to construct an entire portfolio here, especially as things constantly change. However, see below for example, the portfolio we built as a class at Columbia University's Earth Institute.

TABLE 3. Earth Institute portfolio, 2009

Ticker	Company	2009 returns
US equity		
AMZN	Amazon.com	+166%
AXP	American Express	+121%
AAPL	Apple	+149%
AMAT	Applied Materials	+39%
KO	Coca-Cola	+29%
FSLR	First Solar	-3%
GPS	Gap Inc.	+58%
GE	General Electric	-7%
IBM	Intl Business Machines	+59%
ITRI	Itron Inc.	+7%
JCI	Johnson Controls	+53%
PLL	Pall Corp	+29%
TTEK	Tetra Tech	+15%
WMT	Walmart	-4%
Non-US equity		
0494	Li & Fung (HK)	+129%
RHAYY	Rhodia (France)	+181%

As we found at the end of 2009,[34] these companies returned +63% as an aggregate portfolio in 2009 versus the S&P 500's +25%, for an outperformance of 252%, and went on to outperform benchmarks the following year as well.

Some caveats. Such portfolios naturally need to be actively managed – this example is indicative only, and holes can be poked in any such portfolio. There are companies we liked at the time which we would now not include. Much as it was a darling at the time, First Solar in the list above, for example, we would obviously have sold long ago. So a keen eye always needs to be kept on chosen investments. Yale University, a heralded leader in endowment investing, listed Suntech as a positive sustainable investment in a recent report.[35] (It is not clear from an annual snapshot whether Yale held on through the company's eventual bankruptcy, or sold off at some point – so occasional glances at portfolios only have so much utility.)

The US figures to be a leader in sustainable innovation. We recommend half the companies come from this part of the world, Europe another 25%, and another 25% from the rest of the world. Large cap companies look likely to be able to scale the changes required, and will be under increasing internal and external pressure to do so. Large caps should be 80% or so of the portfolio, with smaller companies chosen more carefully. Always be careful of overvaluation. Price targets should be set in advance and adhered to.

Most importantly, you should get to know companies closely, and try and get ahead of the market by spotting trends in advance. Who can scale cheap Chinese solar? Which US companies are working feverishly on sustainability but haven't announced it, or choose to keep it relatively quiet? Which companies can scale a great innovation and are actively seeking such opportunities? Conversely, which companies are incapable of executing even if they have a great idea, and to what degree has the market gotten ahead of some exciting ideas? These are all critical considerations.

There should also be an expectation of change. When you look at the lists of the largest companies in the world over time, there isn't a lot of consistency. Companies come and go. The same will be true of sustainable investing.

Back in our first book, we performed an analysis of the most owned companies by sustainable investing minded portfolios globally, and found the following were most commonly owned: Abengoa, Aviva, BT, Canadian Hydro, Canon, Conergy, Gamesa, Geberit, ING, Itron, Nokia, Novozymes, SolarWorld, Veolia Environnement and Vestas Wind Systems. A number of these companies hit hard times, and in fact, there are few if any outperforming names in that list. The reasons for this are many, but are especially rooted in the following trends that played out. First, anticipated global negotiations headed up by the UN that culminated in Copenhagen did not lead to a resulting price on carbon. Second, the financial crisis of 2008 hit budgets hard, making the need for a business model imperative, and reducing the margins for error in the process. Third, we largely had a cleantech bubble burst at the same time. Alternative energy and other efficiency plays have largely been much like the biotech experience – a few winners, many losers. The same dynamic has played out in private equity. Vinod Khosla, for example, fully expects 90% of his investments in this space to fail, while in search of the next Google. Much of the private equity/venture capital story is still playing out, with much damage having occurred in the process, and not all of it yet visible.

Constructing a sustainable portfolio requires more of a keen eye on bubble formation than was applied in the past. Investing in the manner above, over and under weighting key sectors, angling towards large cap companies, focusing on regions such as the US that are driving change, looking for companies reporting revenue around sustainability, and keeping one eye always on the business model are all essential. Use of existing ESG data is recommended, but with the very big caveat that such data are almost by definition retrospective, and therefore not indicative of future growth potential from sustainability. Few if any analysts are doing a comprehensive job on this. ESG data can help spot companies like BP that had hundreds of recent violations leading up to the Deepwater Horizon crisis, or can also spot financial services companies like Bear Stearns and Lehman Brothers that did not have adequate checks and balances in place from a governance perspective. This is all very helpful information, but it doesn't provide you with a clear picture of where we are headed on opportunity.

Parnassus Equity & Income Fund

Parnassus Equity & Income Fund, as mentioned, has been the fastest growing SRI fund in the US, and perhaps the world, rising to now manage well over $6B in equity. You can see their top 10 holdings in Table 4 (overleaf), representing over 37% of their holdings. These companies represent a mix of technology innovators, manufacturers and others listed in the US, and this portfolio has changed dramatically over time. Back in 2007, before the financial crisis, JPMorgan Chase was their largest holding, and oil and gas companies were about 10% of what was less than $1B in equity holdings overall. Parnassus performed well during the financial crisis, and has succeeded by always keeping a keen

TABLE 4. Parnassus Equity & Income Fund top 10 holdings as of 28 February 2013[36]

Procter & Gamble	4.5%
Applied Materials	4.3%
PepsiCo	4.2%
Teleflex	4.1%
Waste Management	3.9%
Google	3.6%
Questar	3.4%
Charles Schwab	3.2%
Gilead Sciences	3.2%
Pentair	3.0%

eye on the business side of things, while remaining rooted in investing in what they see as companies well positioned for tomorrow.

We remain convinced that with unshakeable trends afoot across sustainability challenges, that positioning yourself in a sustainable manner will shield your portfolios from downside risks and price pressures, while allowing you to ride the megatrend of our time through the companies that want to, and can, drive the changes we require. There are clear examples emerging of ways to outperform in the process.

Conclusion

REGARDLESS OF THE PERSONAL PREFERENCES stated above, the 'climate cliff' and other environmental factors from across resource constraints, oceanic health, fresh water and biodiversity loom as trump cards for a future healthy society and economy. These are of course all interconnected, as environmental issues are connected with social realities and governance overrides both environment and social concerns, as practice and business infrastructure, which can help solve or ignore these problems, in effect locking E, S and G together systemically.

What could emerge as an answer is an extension of investment trends from active to more passive investing, but instead steered into a more sustainable roadmapped future along a specific transition plan. Low cost funds, chiefly exchange traded funds (ETFs), have emerged as appealing to investors who want to minimize their expenses. If applied at scale, such a solution could be the 'Walmartization of Wall Street'. This could be applied across asset allocation models, across all categories of assets owned. The risks of not doing something like this are too great, and the benefits of doing otherwise are likewise becoming murky to say the least. Examples of how this could be performed include changing weightings on sectors over time into what could lead us through this transition. For example, coal companies need not be owned. Oil and gas companies could be included, but under certain conditions, for example, that they transition their fuel mix over time towards what we as a global society require, not only for our near-term energy needs, but for future generations as well. Other asset classes have great importance, especially as public equity continues its global struggle to find growth in a low growth world. Many different efforts also are burgeoning around the ideas of crowdsourcing impact investing and other means of implementing green infrastructure at scale, either on a project or portfolio basis. It would behoove global asset owners to band together to find ways to collaborate on such an agenda. Mosaic, a new startup company, seeks solar investment through crowdfunding, and sold out its first allocation. A form of shared economy through social media/internet which involves not only energy sourcing, but also investing, remains another trend to follow closely, as individuals seek ways of matching their money and expenditure to the end results they desire for their communities and families.

A transition plan, broadly mapped across assets to solution could also help avoid what some call 'predictable surprises'.[37] In *Evolutions in Sustainable Investing*, for example, we highlighted how Domini avoided investing in BP. When launching a new international fund, Domini for the first time needed to look beyond US borders, and via an analysis of accidents and safety violations, decided against investing in BP, which looks prescient after the Gulf of Mexico spill. We also reviewed in our previous book the engagement and advocacy efforts of the likes of Calvert and NEI. Such efforts are a critical component of the checks and balances that financial systems require for their own health, and those checks and balances are not robust enough at present.

Other trends raise awareness on these issues, such as the Do The Math tour of 350.org, encouraging students to ask their universities to divest from fossil fuels. While not a sophisticated answer (see my two

66

recent articles on this at www.greenbiz.com),[38,39] it seems unlikely that pressures on business as usual will subside anytime soon.

Of further interest are the sorts of positive, opportunities-focused solutions that can emerge as viable and profitable. In a previous book, I reviewed dMass (**www.dmass.net**), a theory around dematerialization as one more path to the sorts of innovation and efficiency that companies can gain from. Biomimicry is emerging as an exciting technique, finding ways that nature has proven to be a most efficient and elegant closed loop, and bringing that to scale as well. It may become an important consideration for investors in the times ahead. It is exciting to see new technologies and techniques from dMass to biomimicry and beyond emerge. A sustainable future is most likely to emerge from innovative thinking, and so investment at scale to encourage these sorts of innovative strategies is badly needed, to help move us from what might be called our current 'stasis quo'. It is time to find the companies who can lead the transition we have been speaking of, and in effect 'Buy Right and Hold' for a sustainable future. We need the Warren Buffett of sustainable investing to emerge, at scale, who can be mimicked and lead the way forward.

Benchmark investing on a march to an unsustainable status quo is not a way to fulfill one's fiduciary duty, nor a way to maximize potential returns over the long term if there is no sustainable future that would result. Performance in the status quo is now poor at best, if the last 12 years of US benchmark performance tells us anything. Global investing is in many ways overpowered by indexes plagued by sticking with 'universal ownership' of all sectors, creating an unwitting systemic obstacle to needed change. In some ways, the only solution may be to pull out the carpet with one, swift strong tug. A better way would be to build a roadmap to a transition plan, and reward companies, public and private, who help lead the way in a positive manner.

As externalities become either inevitably internalized or experienced, chasing alpha with tunnel vision is no longer the best approach to maximizing returns in a fruitless chase for the returns of days gone by. Shockingly, although we are very much in an age of increased transparency, all-time high levels of market inefficiency somehow still abound around so-called externalities, and at some point, as George Soros held in *The Alchemy of Finance* some time ago, everything eventually seeks its level of true value.

Even if there is only a correlation between well run companies that end up outperforming and those that need to manage their sustainability risks and opportunities successfully, that's fine, especially if one cannot be achieved without the other. Nothing ever quite plays out as we might expect in investing, though the mainstreaming of sustainability in this regard is certainly likely in a resource challenged world with increasing human population fully expected. Winners will come from those who can innovate or build maximum efficiencies and related revenue and savings accordingly. Ultimately, whether we are talking about innovation or efficiency, we are talking about change. And therefore, the companies that can create and drive the changes we require through innovation and efficiency successfully will win. Those that don't change with the times will be left behind and fail. Business as usual becomes the clearest possible recipe for failure for both companies and asset owners alike. This becomes the critical way to measure companies and fund managers. This dynamic will help us solve the sustainability challenges of our time, and the sooner we all recognize this, the better.

The history of business is lined with companies who did not capitalize on trends, instead deciding to stay in what all too often turns out to be a temporary comfort zone, from the British East India Company to Eastman Kodak and Xerox. Staying ahead of demographics with global needs and desires in mind will lead to all sorts of positive opportunities. Demonstrate that you have found more revenue through sustainability than the market perceives, and you will not only win, but create a positive dynamic that benefits all stakeholders. While we ultimately don't know exactly what and where the tipping points are, there will be major problems if we stick with business as usual. We will go through a major transition either driven by ignorance, or through meaningful, designed transformation. Assuming we would prefer to transition successfully, sustainable investing offers the best chance for that success via assets deployed at scale that in effect forces best corporate practice through a race for capital. If this is our best chance, then we need asset owners to take to this en masse as soon as possible. This would then result in corporates and investors best positioned to become the most likely winners of tomorrow. Getting ahead of this trend now therefore becomes the most significant investment and business opportunity of our time.

....

Notes

1. Krosinsky, C. 2013. *The State of Ownership*. At **www.sustainablefinancial markets.net**, March.

2. http://books.google.com/books?id=r4YtDGq7lTOC&pg=PA5&lpg=PA5& dq=krosinsky+viederman+ottawa&source=bl&ots=iMBOGodNkO&sig=5lI PxmwuW4JTFo-MB-uxq1N1d78&hl=en&sa=X&ei=ODRPUY65Ns_B4AOH-oDQCA&ved=0CDIQ6AEwAQ#v=onepage&q=krosinsky%20viederman%20 ottawa&f=false

3. Unburnable Carbon 2011, www.carbontracker.org

4. Meadows, D. 1972. *The Limits to Growth* (New York: New York University Press).

5. Robins, N. 2006. *The Corporation that Changed the World: How the East India Company Shaped the Modern Multinational* (London: Pluto Press).

6. http://www.rijpm.com/pre_reading_files/Mark_Van_Clieaf_Pre-Reading_ May_2011.pdf

7. Viederman, S. 2008. Fiduciary duty. In: Krosinsky, C. and Robins, N. (eds) *Sustainable Investing: The Art of Long Term Performance*, pp. 189–200 (London: Earthscan).

8. Gunther, M. 2012. *Suck It Up: How Capturing Carbon from the Air Can Help Solve the Climate Crisis* (Kindle Single).

9. http://en.wikipedia.org/wiki/History_of_slavery

10. http://www.simmons-simmons.com/docs/an_introduction_to_islamic_ finance.pdf

11. Krosinsky, C. and Robins, N. (eds). 2008. *Sustainable Investing: The Art of Long Term Performance* (London: Earthscan).

12. Krosinsky, C., Robins, N. and Viederman, S. (eds). 2011. *Evolutions in Sustainable Investing: Strategies, Funds, and Thought Leadership* (Hoboken, NJ: Wiley).

13. Concordia webinar, March 2013. Lussier, J. 2013. *Successful Investing is a Process: Structuring Efficient Portfolios for Outperformance* (Hoboken, NJ: Wiley).

14. Krosinsky et al. (eds), *Evolutions in Sustainable Investing.*

15. Sucher, S.J., Beyersdorfer, D. and Jensen, A.D. 2009. Generation Investment Management. Harvard Business School Technology & Operations Mgt Unit Paper No. 1404584, September.

16. http://www.jupiteronline.com/Individual-investors/Funds-and-prices/Jupiter-Ecology-Fund–MH02?tab=portfoliostatistics

17. See the 'SIF Trends Report 2010', a pay-for report available here http://www.ussif.org/. A related article on the content of that report can be found here http://www.tellus.org/publications/files/voorhes-humphreys-recent-trends-joi-2011.pdf

18. www.socialinvest.org using data from Bloomberg.

19. http://www.parnassus.com/parnassus-mutual-funds/equity-income/investor-shares/Portfolio.aspx

20. http://www.portfolio21.com/fund/snapshot/

21. Krosinsky et al. (eds), *Evolutions in Sustainable Investing* provides greater detail than a short eBook such as this can provide, with much more on fund managers and strategists and the methods they deploy, including a longer piece on Portfolio 21, Generation, Jupiter Ecology and other fund managers from Sustainable Asset Management, Calvert and Domini, etc.

22. Krosinsky and Robins, *Sustainable Investing.*

23. http://www.parnassus.com/our-firm/highlight.aspx?hl=57

24. http://www.greenbiz.com/news/2010/01/04/resolution-new-decade-sustainability-and-investing

25. http://www.unepfi.org/fileadmin/documents/universal_ownership_full.pdf

26. http://www.pwc.com/gx/en/sustainability/publications/low-carbon-economy-index/index.jhtml

27. http://www.greenbiz.com/blog/2013/01/04/investing-strategy-climate-change

28. http://www.iea.org/etp/

29. http://www.unglobalcompact.org/aboutthegc/thetenprinciples/index.html

30. http://www.theiirc.org/resources-2/framework-development/prototype-international-framework-working-draft/

31. http://www.sustainabilityprofessionals.org/system/files/LEXICON_McElroy_SustainableLifeMedia.pdf

32. http://www.msci.com/resources/factsheets/index_fact_sheet/msci-world-index.pdf

33. http://www.msci.com/products/indices/country_and_regional/em/

34. http://www.greenbiz.com/news/2010/01/04/resolution-new-decade-sustainability-and-investing

35. http://investments.yale.edu/images/documents/Yale_Endowment_09.pdf

36. http://www.parnassus.com/parnassus-mutual-funds/equity-income/investor-shares/Portfolio.aspx

37. http://preventablesurprises.com/resources/articles/

38. http://www.greenbiz.com/blog/2012/11/19/do-math-tour-doesnt-add-up

39. http://www.greenbiz.com/blog/2013/01/04/investing-strategy-climate-change

For Product Safety Concerns and Information please contact our EU
representative GPSR@taylorandfrancis.com
Taylor & Francis Verlag GmbH, Kaufingerstraße 24, 80331 München, Germany

www.ingramcontent.com/pod-product-compliance
Ingram Content Group UK Ltd.
Pitfield, Milton Keynes, MK11 3LW, UK
UKHW040928180425
457613UK00011B/286